Thomas Doucet
Hero of Plaisance

© 2004 Susan Chalker Browne
Artwork © 2004 Heather Maloney

Le Conseil des Arts | The Canada Council
du Canada | for the Arts

We acknowledge the support of The Canada Council for the Arts for our publishing program.

We acknowledge the financial support of the Government of Canada through the Book Publishing Industry Development Program (BPIDP) for our publishing program.

All rights reserved. No part of this work covered by the copyrights hereon may be reproduced or used in any form or by any means—graphic, electronic or mechanical—without the prior written permission of the publisher. Any requests for photocopying, recording, taping or information storage and retrieval systems of any part of this book shall be directed in writing to the Canadian Reprography Collective,
One Yonge Street, Suite 1900, Toronto, Ontario M5E 1E5.

Cover Art by Heather Maloney
Cover Design by Todd Manning
Printed on acid-free paper

Published by
TUCKAMORE BOOKS
an imprint of CREATIVE BOOK PUBLISHING
a Transcontinental Inc. associated company
P.O. Box 8660, St. John's, Newfoundland A1B 3T7

First Printing November 2004

Typeset in 14 point Times New Roman

Printed in Canada by:
Transcontinental Inc.

National Library of Canada Cataloguing in Publication

Browne, Susan Chalker, 1958-
    Thomas Doucet, hero of Plaisance / written by Susan Chalker Browne ; illustrated by Heather Maloney.

ISBN 1-894294-76-9

    1. Iberville's Expedition to Newfoundland, 1696--Juvenile fiction.
2. Avalon Peninsula (N.L.)--History--Juvenile fiction. I. Maloney, Heather
II. Title.

PS8553.R691T46 2004   jC813'.6   C2004-906564-5

Thomas Doucet
Hero of Plaisance

Written by
Susan Chalker Browne

Illustrated by
Heather Maloney

Tuckamore Books
St. John's, Newfoundland and Labrador
2004

For Paul.
— SCB

For my mother.
— HM

Chapter One

September 12, 1696

The noonday sun glinted off the water and Thomas Doucet shielded his eyes from the glare. Around him, codfish—split, salted and drying—spread out in all directions. The smell of it surrounded him like a fog.

"Boy! Over here!" a ruddy-faced man bellowed from farther down the beach. Thomas sighed. His master was a harsh one. A moment of idleness would never be overlooked. "These fish need turning," called the beach master. "I'm not paying you to look at the ocean."

Thomas trudged along the beach and began to turn the fish. Dry side to the bottom, damp side to the sun and the air. His hands were red and sore from the salt on the fish, but he knew he was lucky to have this work. Papa was not as strong as he used to be and mama needed his help. Still, he couldn't help thinking of his friend Nicolas Chevalier, at that very moment doing lessons with the Recollet Fathers. But Nicolas was the son of a man who owned five fishing boats, and that made all the difference.

Thomas looked around at the pebbled beach that stretched into the sea like a tongue. Green hills rose from the water, sheltering the exposed land. 'I never think of France anymore,' he thought. 'I guess Plaisance is home now.'

Wooden cabins scattered along the ribbon of rock and gravel; forty families lived in the colony year round. The best house belonged to the governor and only the finest food was ever served there. The Recollet Fathers ran the church and taught the sons of rich men. Soldiers from Fort Royal were sometimes seen in the settlement, and traveling Mi'kmaq were occasionally spotted in the woods. During the fishing season the population ballooned, as ships arrived from France carrying workers. Sometimes ships sailed in from Boston with food and supplies. Yes, there was always something happening in Plaisance.

"Well, what's this?" said the beach master, who stood facing the sea. The entire shore crew looked up. Cleanly outlined on the horizon was a large vessel, flags flapping from its tall masts.

"It's the *Envieux*!" shouted Lamontagne, the salter who had been working next to Thomas. "D'Iberville's ship—he's arrived!" he cried, dropping his bucket of salt.

D'Iberville! Excitement surged through Thomas and he jumped to his feet. Pierre Le Moyne Sieur D'Iberville, the hero of New France, a legend unto himself. For weeks it had been rumoured he was coming to Plaisance. People said he would drive the English from Newfoundland, claiming the island—and its treasure of codfish—for France.

The beach master stared at the approaching ship, his hand rubbing the stubble on his chin. "That man is as fearless crossing mountains and rivers as he is upon the sea."

"I'll fight with D'Iberville," said Lamontagne in a low, determined voice. "We'll toss the English out and take all of Newfoundland for France."

Thomas Doucet glanced at the beach master who didn't seem to have heard, then looked back at the salter in wonder. Lamontagne was so lucky. 'When I'm older,' Thomas vowed to himself, 'I too will fight for D'Iberville and France.'

Chapter Two

September 13, 1696

Thomas and Nicolas sat on the wharf, watching the *Envieux* dip and sway in the offshore waves. "Have you seen him yet, Nicolas?" asked Thomas. "What's he like?"

"He visited my father this morning," said Nicolas. "He asked him to join the campaign to rid Newfoundland of the English."

"Will your father fight?" asked Thomas, his eyes wide. "Will he go with D'Iberville?"

"Of course! Papa is very strong and brave. But nobody knows when the campaign will begin. D'Iberville is furious that only four days ago the governor left Plaisance with a fleet of vessels and men. He's gone to fight the English on his own, but he was supposed to wait for D'Iberville—they were to attack together. Now D'Iberville says that plan is ruined. The English will know the French are coming and they will be ready for us."

"Why doesn't he leave right away and catch up with Governor De Brouillan?" Thomas asked. "D'Iberville is fast and clever. He could do that."

"He would if he had enough men and supplies, but he doesn't. The ships carrying his soldiers and food haven't arrived. Now he must wait for those ships to come to Plaisance and for De Brouillan to return." Nicolas turned toward his friend and opened his palm. "Look what he gave me!" It was a small silver cross.

Thomas couldn't believe his eyes. "D'Iberville gave you that? He actually spoke to you?"

"I was amazed," said Nicolas, smiling at the memory. "I was sitting in the corner listening. I couldn't stop staring at the sword hanging from his side and the silver buckles on his shoes. He never even looked in my direction. But on his way out the door, he stopped and gave me this. He said in a few years I could fight with him, too. And I will. As soon as I'm sixteen."

"Thomas! There you are!" The two boys turned as Madeleine Doucet climbed up on the wharf. Fair hair curled around her face. Her cheeks were pink with excitement and her brown eyes glowed. "You'll never guess what! I just passed Sieur D'Iberville on the road and he looked at me and smiled! Oh and before I forget, Mama says you're to come at once to chop some wood." She plopped down on the wharf next to her brother. "Papa's feeling poorly again and he can't do it."

Thomas flushed with embarrassment. Here was Nicolas's father ready to fight with D'Iberville, while his own papa had not enough strength to chop wood.

"Did D'Iberville speak to you, Madeleine?" asked Nicolas, glancing at Thomas.

"Oh, no! He was far too busy to speak to me. He's rounding up men for his campaign against the English. And he's looking for food and supplies from the garrison, because he hasn't any of his own. That's what Mali tells me anyway."

Mali was a young Mi'kmaw girl who lived with her family in the woods just outside Plaisance. They had recently set up camp there so the men could hunt caribou and trap beaver. Mali and Madeleine had met by the river, and now got together whenever they could steal a few minutes from their chores. Madeleine knew a few Mi'kmaq words and Mali understood some French; still it always amazed Thomas how much the girls were able to tell each other.

"How does Mali know all this?" asked Thomas.

"Her papa heard it from the Indians traveling with D'Iberville!" said Madeleine. "D'Iberville greatly admires the Indians for their skill and silence in the woods. Mali says they will fight with him, too."

Thomas's stomach sank even further. Everyone, it seemed, was being favoured by D'Iberville. Everyone except Thomas and his papa.

Chapter Three

October 17, 1696

Thomas's mother forked a carrot from the pot and shook her head at it. "Nothing can grow in this God-forsaken place," she said. "The soil's so thin and the wind so fierce. We should have never left France."

Thomas shoveled another spoonful of fish stew into his mouth and mopped up the broth with bread. Small or not, the carrots tasted good to him. But he knew better than to challenge his mother. Everything made her angry these days.

"That's all I can eat right now, my dear," said Thomas's father, from his chair by the fire. He handed his plate over. It was still full of food.

"George! You must finish your supper! How can you return to Fort Royal tomorrow with nothing in your stomach?" Jeanne Doucet's voice was sharp, her face creased with worry.

"I'll be fine in the morning. Rest is what I need right now." George Doucet closed his eyes and settled his chin on his chest.

Thomas and Madeleine stopped eating and looked at each

other. Their father had not been the same since construction began on Fort Royal several years ago. He had been pushing a large rock up the hill when it rolled back over him, crushing his leg. Recovery had been slow, and ever since the accident, George Doucet walked with a limp. Still, each day he returned to Fort Royal, doing odd jobs for the soldiers.

"Those officers in the garrison will work a man into the grave," muttered Jeanne Doucet. "And then where will we be?"

A shiver ran through Thomas at his mother's words. "Papa," he said, a little too loudly. "Did you hear about Governor De Brouillan? How he attacked the English?"

George Doucet opened one eye. "Do you forget, my son, that I was at Fort Royal this afternoon? I saw the governor's ships sail into the harbour."

"Yes, but did you hear how he burnt the English out of Bay Bulls?" continued Thomas, desperate to draw his father into conversation. "And how he tried to take St. John's, but failed?"

Thomas had his father's attention now. George Doucet sat up straight. "What have you heard?" he asked his son.

"That Governor De Brouillan burnt the houses in Ferryland and sent one hundred and fifty English back to England. That he burned all the houses in Bay Bulls and forced the English captain there to set fire to his own ship. But he

couldn't enter the harbour at St. John's. It was too heavily guarded."

"And I heard," said Madeleine, tossing her hair, "that D'Iberville is furious with the governor. He says De Brouillan was a fool to try to take St. John's by sea. He says the only way to do it is by land, to sneak up behind the English while their eyes are on the ocean. And he says it must be done in winter, when the English in St. John's think they're safe."

Thomas and George Doucet stared at Madeleine. Even Jeanne Doucet turned toward her daughter from her spot at the hearth. "Madeleine, my child, where have you heard all this?"

"Let me guess," said Thomas. "From Mali?"

Madeleine smiled, delighted with the attention. "Mali's papa hears everything from the Indians traveling with D'Iberville."

George Doucet leaned his elbows on his knees and looked into the fire. "What I heard is that each man wants to be leader. Governor De Brouillan says he's in charge because he's the king's representative in Newfoundland. But D'Iberville has letters of commission from Governor Frontenac of New France, as well as from the king."

Jeanne Doucet snorted in disgust. "I'd say they're fighting over who gets the spoils when the battles are done. Those two are more concerned with lining their own pockets. If they can't decide who's in charge there'll be no further attacks on the English. And we might as well wait for the English to come to Plaisance and drive us all away."

Chapter Four

November 1, 1696

Fog shrouded the hills; underfoot the beach rocks were slick with moisture. Thomas, Madeleine and Nicolas huddled together in the chill. Around them the crowd shuffled and murmured, all eyes on the governor's house.

"Well, those two seem to have patched up their differences," said one old man. "D'Iberville's in the governor's house, while the governor has left on D'Iberville's ship."

"Last week it looked hopeless," whispered Nicolas to Thomas. "Papa says the Indians refused to fight with the governor and that D'Iberville himself threatened to sail for France."

"How did they work it out?" asked Thomas.

"D'Iberville needed the governor's men, and they both needed the supplies that arrived on D'Iberville's ships. They were forced to work with each other."

On the other side of the beach stood a small group of Mi'kmaq women and children. Madeleine spotted Mali and the two girls smiled and waved at each other. Mali's shiny black braids were as long as her arms, her tunic glimmered with coloured beads.

"Mali's papa says D'Iberville will march through the woods," said Madeleine. "Governor De Brouillan has already left by ship and they'll all meet up in Ferryland."

"That's right," said Nicolas, smiling at Madeleine. "From there they'll plan their attack on St. John's."

Suddenly, there was the sound of a drum rolling, and the front door of the governor's house opened wide. "There he is!" shouted a child, as Pierre Le Moyne D'Iberville stepped out into the gravel road. Brass buttons gleamed on his long blue coat, while the white feather on his hat bounced with every movement. A silver sword swung from his side and a long, dark musket balanced over his shoulder.

The drum continued to beat as from behind the house streamed dozens of men: those traveling with D'Iberville, plus the men of Plaisance. "There's Papa!" shouted Nicolas, as the men marched to the beach.

"Look!" cried Madeleine, pointing to a warrior in a fur-lined robe. Even Lamontagne the salter strutted proudly, a fife in his hands.

Thomas Doucet bit his lip in shame. He thought of his own father, without the energy to rise from his bed, no longer able to climb the hill to Fort Royal. He remembered waking last night to the sound of deep hacking coughs, and in between, the sound of his mother's urgent whispers.

Suddenly the drumming ceased and a small man in black moved to the centre of the crowd. "That's Father

Baudoin," Nicolas told Thomas. "He's traveling with D'Iberville."

The priest opened a little book and began to pray. "May the Lord guide us on our journey and protect us from the enemy." His voice was as small and thin as the man himself. The crowd hushed and leaned forward to listen.

With the last "Amen," the drum rolled again and the fife played high and bright. D'Iberville and his soldiers climbed into their boats and paddled across the water to the wooded hills beyond Plaisance.

"That's the last we'll likely see of them!" huffed an old man to his wife. "A winter campaign! They'll all be frozen in their sleep!"

"There's already snow in the woods," said another. "And ice on the road in the mornings."

Nicolas stared at the old men, but Thomas grabbed his arm. "Don't listen to them," he said. "D'Iberville has fought in winter before. Your papa will be safe with him."

Chapter Five

December 2, 1696

The air was muffled and still as Madeleine Doucet tramped along on her snowshoes. Their soft swoosh-swoosh was the only sound in the woods. She breathed deeply, letting the cool cleanness fill her lungs. It felt so good to be away from home.

With each day that passed her papa grew weaker and her mama more irritable. She knew her mama was worn out from work, but still her moods were difficult to bear. She thought back to yesterday and the syrup of goat's milk, eggs and rum that mama had heated over the fire and spooned into papa's mouth. How the mixture had brightened papa for a while, but then by evening he was feverish again. And how mama had snapped at her to go feed the chickens and make herself useful.

Which is why this morning she had suggested that maybe some spruce tea, the kind the Mi'kmaq brewed, might be the very thing for papa. The dullness in mama's eyes had lifted then, and she quickly agreed. And now Madeleine found herself heading toward the camp where Mali lived with her family.

Mali and her parents were so kind to Madeleine. She knew they would be happy to help. Even the snowshoes on her feet were a gift from the Mi'kmaw family. *Aqam*—that was their word for snowshoe. And they were lighter and faster than the pair her papa had made. Somehow the Mi'kmaq seemed to better understand these things.

She rounded a corner on the path and immediately the Mi'kmaw camp came into view. Sheltered by fir trees, the winter wigwams nestled into the ground, evergreen boughs and snow packed up against the sides. Birchbark canoes rested on the riverbank. Several women gathered around a fire in the centre of the camp. Nearby some children laughed and chased each other.

"Madeleine?" Mali ran toward her friend, her eyes questioning.

"My papa. He's sick," said Madeleine, using her hands to explain. "Spruce tea. He needs spruce tea."

Mali seemed to understand. She pulled Madeleine toward her mother, one of the women by the fire. Mali spoke to her mother, who looked at Madeleine for a moment then disappeared into the woods.

"Yes," Mali said, smiling. She squeezed Madeleine's hand. "Spruce tea."

Soon Mali's mother returned with a jug and a small pouch of caribou hide. She pressed both into Madeleine's arms, then turned and spoke rapidly to her daughter, who listened intently.

"Boil roots," Mali said to Madeleine. Then she beat her fist into her hand and rubbed the hand in a circle on her chest.

Madeleine understood. A poultice for her father's chest to help dissolve the cough. "Thank you," she said, smiling at Mali's mother who nodded her head solemnly.

Madeleine linked her arm with Mali's. "Walk with me?" she asked. Mali looked at her mother, who spoke urgently to her daughter. Madeleine thought she heard *sipu*, the Mi'kmaw word for river.

"Ice," said Mali, as the two girls turned toward the woods. And again Madeleine understood. Be careful of the ice on the river, the Mi'kmaw mother had warned. Be careful of thin ice.

Chapter Six

December 11, 1696

Thomas Doucet braced his back against the bitter wind that cut across the side of the hill. His mittened hands placed another rock upon the wall, while the soldier beside him slapped mortar on it with a trowel. In a few days the wall would be high enough to offer some protection from the winter wind. Until then, thought Thomas, his cheeks would continue to sting with the cold.

An officer stopped by the pair and surveyed their work. "Not bad," he growled. "Make sure these rocks are lined up evenly." He glared at Thomas and moved on down the line.

Thomas sighed. The garrison had been good to give him this work at Fort Royal, but many of the men resented his presence. "A boy doing a man's job," they muttered to each other. But the officer in charge had hired him after Thomas's father became too sick to work. Thomas knew that to prove himself he must toil twice as hard as anyone else.

He pulled at another big rock and heaved it onto the wall. This was a smaller lookout, farther down the hill from the main fort. Originally built with wooden pickets, it was now being reinforced with mortar and stone. Some said the

orders for reinforcement came directly from Governor De Brouillan himself.

How were they doing, Thomas wondered. How was the winter campaign going? There wasn't a bit of news since D'Iberville left with his soldiers on All Saints Day. But the snow and the cold had come early this year, and all the old men of Plaisance shook their heads at the foolishness of D'Iberville's plan.

'Nicolas must be worried about his papa,' thought Thomas, who hadn't seen much of his friend since starting work at the fort. Each morning, Thomas was up before dawn to paddle across the water, and then scale the hill to Fort Royal. By the time he returned home each evening, it was dark again. He had only the strength to eat his supper and fall into bed.

At least, thought Thomas, his own papa was feeling a bit better. The fever had left him and he was able to sit by the fire for part of each day. His skin was still white and he tired easily, but Thomas now felt sure that papa would survive the winter. He didn't know whether it was the spruce tea or the roots in the leather pouch, but something had worked a cure. Mama had called it a miracle.

"Well, what's this?" said the soldier beside Thomas. "Some boats approaching!" Thomas stood up and peered at the harbour. Behind him, the commanding officer positioned himself with his spyglass.

"I see Lemar and there's Trotel. They all left with

D'Iberville last month. Why are they returning on their own?"

Thomas's stomach churned with a mixture of excitement and dread. Finally some news of the campaign!

Chapter Seven

December 12, 1696

Wrapped inside a wool blanket, George Doucet huddled close to the fire. Before him, a small chicken roasted on a spit inside the hearth, its sizzling aroma filling the small cabin. "Keep turning the chicken, Madeleine," ordered Jeanne Doucet, "unless you like it burnt on one side and raw on the other."

Suddenly the front door opened and Thomas stepped in from the darkness, stamping the snow from his boots. "Mama! Papa! Have you heard? D'Iberville has taken St. John's!"

"Taken St. John's?" George Doucet turned from the fire, his eyes bright with interest. "Where did you hear this?"

"From the soldiers at the fort," Thomas said breathlessly. "On November twenty-sixth there was a fierce battle in some burnt woods just outside St. John's. The English heard the French were approaching and sent out soldiers to stop them. D'Iberville attacked them fiercely and chased them over the Southside Hills into St. John's. They say D'Iberville ran so fast that Governor De Brouillan couldn't keep up with him."

"What happened then?" asked Jeanne Doucet, her bread

knife motionless over the loaf on the table.

"Well, some of the English jumped on a ship and sailed through the Narrows just in time. The rest of them crowded into King William's Fort and barricaded themselves. They were there for two days and two nights, without food or drink or firewood."

"How did D'Iberville get them out?" asked Madeleine, from her spot by the chicken on the spit.

"They attacked a settler called William Drew," said Thomas slowly, eyeing his mother, "and sent him into the fort, bleeding and stumbling. The English weren't long giving up after that."

"They did what?" cried Madeleine, forgetting to crank the spit.

"Oh, the brutes!" said Jeanne Doucet. "To treat another human being like an animal!" She shook the bread knife at her daughter. "Madeleine! The chicken!"

Thomas and his papa looked at each other guiltily. "Sometimes, my dear," said George Doucet, "terrible deeds must be done to win a war."

"Hmmph!" snorted Jeanne Doucet, angrily slicing at the loaf of bread.

"Well, that's what the soldiers were saying today at the fort," ended Thomas quietly.

"Thomas," said Madeleine after a moment, "have you heard about Nicolas Chevalier's papa?"

"No," said Thomas quickly. "Is he hurt?"

"He was injured in the fighting outside St. John's," said Madeleine, "and sent back home along with some other men from Plaisance. They say he has a wound to the stomach and that he's very weak."

Thomas remembered the small boats sailing into the harbour yesterday; they must have been carrying home the injured. "Poor Nicolas," said Thomas. "He must be worried about his papa."

"Thomas," said George Doucet. "What happens now? Where does D'Iberville's campaign go from here?"

"The soldiers say the plan is to burn St. John's to the ground. Every last flake and shed. They say Governor De Brouillan will soon return to Plaisance and that D'Iberville and his men will travel on through the woods. They mean to take Brigus and Port de Grave and Carbonear. D'Iberville is as comfortable with the ice and snow as we are here in our cabin. No Englishman will be safe from him."

Chapter Eight

March 6, 1697

Thomas and Nicolas tramped over the hard-packed snow on their snowshoes, ice-fishing sticks in their hands. It was one of those rare occasions when both boys had a free day. Thomas was not needed at Fort Royal and Nicolas had no lessons with the Recollet Fathers. Thomas's mama had released him from his chores, but was expecting fresh fish to fry for supper. Thomas could almost smell it now, sizzling golden brown in the butter.

"I hear D'Iberville arrived back last night," said Thomas. "What news have you heard?"

"He was in to see papa first thing this morning," said Nicolas, "to see how his wound was healing and tell him about the campaign. Do you know that D'Iberville, Father Baudoin and five other men left Heart's Content on March first and made it to Plaisance yesterday? That's fifty miles in four days! And through the roughest kind of country! There's nothing that man can't do."

"Why is he returning?" asked Thomas. "Is the campaign ended?"

"Not yet. D'Iberville is looking for news and reinforcements from France. But with the ice in Plaisance Harbour

frozen solid, no ships will arrive anytime soon."

"What about the campaign? Are we winning or losing?"

"Winning!" replied Nicolas, with a triumphant grin. "D'Iberville is fearless. First they burned St. John's to the ground and scattered the English from Renews to Torbay. Now they've attacked Carbonear, Old Perlican and Bay de Verde. They've burned Port de Grave, Harbour Grace and Brigus. Everywhere they go, the French flag is left flying."

"How do they survive in the woods in the winter?" asked Thomas.

"They kill the cows of the English settlers and eat them. Sometimes they sleep in their deserted homes. Often when they come into a settlement the English have already fled. Many are hiding in the woods. More are barricaded on Carbonear Island."

"Carbonear Island?"

"Yes," replied Nicolas. "That's the one place that's defied D'Iberville. Hundreds of English from Carbonear, Harbour Grace and even St. John's have retreated there. They have food and guns and cannons. D'Iberville has tried to take the island, but there's no safe place to land."

"So what's next?" asked Thomas.

"D'Iberville plans to attack settlements in Trinity Bay and eventually Bonavista. And they'll keep trying to capture

Carbonear Island."

"Your papa must be sorry to be missing all the excitement," said Thomas, looking at his friend. Monsieur Chevalier had recovered from his injury and was back to running his business.

"A little," replied Nicolas. "But he says he's too old now, and that fighting is for younger men. At least he saw action last fall."

Thomas thought of his own papa who spent last fall near death. Papa had recovered, but would never be strong enough to work at Fort Royal again or earn a living for his family. He spent his days milking the cows and feeding the chickens. Now it was up to Thomas and his mama to put food on the table. Mama had begun doing laundry for the soldiers at the garrison. Her hands were red and chapped from all the scrubbing, and so were Madeleine's who often had to help.

The boys rounded the path and the river came into view. Its surface was white with ice, but even so, Thomas could hear the sound of water gurgling. Suddenly he heard something else. He stepped out on the ice and looked downstream. A dark shape struggled at the edge of the ice, white frothy water racing behind.

"My God!" he shouted. "It's Mali. She's fallen through the ice!"

Chapter Nine

March 6, 1697

The two boys scrambled along the riverbank, pulling at tree branches, sliding along the ice and jumping over rocks. "Mali! Hold on! We're coming!" shouted Thomas. Behind him, Nicolas struggled to keep pace.

Mali lifted her head and saw the boys approaching. "*Kewji!*" she called weakly. "*Kewji!*"

"She says she's cold!" shouted Thomas, over his shoulder to Nicolas. "Hurry!" He stopped at the point of land closest to where the young Mi'kmaw girl clung to the ice. The ice looked thick and sturdy enough, but Thomas knew it could collapse beneath him. Wildly, he looked around for something long enough to reach Mali. An old pine tree tilted at an angle over the river.

Nicolas finally caught up, panting and puffing. Thomas spied the axe dangling from the pack on his back. "Nicolas, quick! Hand me that axe!" Within seconds, Thomas was hacking at the pine tree, his arms and shoulders strong from months of work at Fort Royal.

"Hold on, Mali!" Thomas shouted again, as a huge arm of the tree splintered and cracked and bounced onto the ice. It lay like an arrow, pointing toward the stranded girl.

"Nicolas," said Thomas, breathless from exertion. "We need help. Run to the Mi'kmaw village."

Nicolas disappeared into the woods, while Thomas edged down the bank and inched along the ice on his belly, grabbing at the tree limb beside him.

"Mali, reach for the tree! Can you reach the tree?"

Mali's arm swept across the ice, frantically clutching at air. Suddenly, she slipped further into the water.

"Hold on!" shouted Thomas desperately. With all his strength, he shoved the big branch across the ice, sliding it nearer the girl. The tip of the tree stopped over the open water, while Thomas clung firmly to the base.

"Grab it!" he ordered.

Mali's arms wrapped around the tree limb. Carefully, Thomas dragged it back toward him. Slowly, the girl's torso emerged from the swirling water. Then her legs. Then she was lying flat on the ice. As soon as Mali was within reach, Thomas grabbed her arm and pulled her to land.

The girl's eyes were half-lidded with the cold, her lips were blue and ice had formed on her eyebrows. She said nothing. Thomas tore off his jacket and wrapped it round her shoulders.

Suddenly, there were voices in the bushes. Several

Mi'kmaq broke through the trees and rushed to the riverbank, Nicolas running behind them. Mali was wrapped in blankets and whisked away through the woods.

One of the Mi'kmaw men remained behind and approached Thomas, his eyes glassy with tears. The old man grasped the boy's shoulder, bowed slightly, and then he too was gone. Nicolas and Thomas were left alone.

"You saved her life!" said Nicolas. "You saved Mali from drowning."

Thomas couldn't speak. He stood on the riverbank, the old pine limb at his feet, his eyes on the broken ice just beyond.

Chapter 10

March 19, 1697

It was a small group that gathered on the beach at Plaisance, waiting for Pierre Le Moyne D'Iberville to set sail. There were no drums or marching this time, no fife playing. D'Iberville was simply rejoining his men at their base camp in Bull Arm. From there they would plan their attack on settlements in Trinity Bay, including Bonavista.

The ice in Plaisance harbour had finally broken up, but still there were no ships from France and D'Iberville was tired of waiting. A small boat bobbed in the water, ready to take him away.

Thomas and Nicolas had agreed to meet on the beach at sunrise, before Thomas left for Fort Royal and Nicolas for his lessons with the Recollet Fathers. But Madeleine had heard of their plan, and also wanted to see D'Iberville leave. Even George Doucet was curious enough to make the trip down to the water, leaning heavily on a thick wooden pole. A dozen other French settlers had also gathered to see the great man off.

Farther down the beach they could see D'Iberville approaching with his party: Father Baudoin and the men who would guide the boat. They barely glanced at the small group on the beach as they strode past.

Suddenly, D'Iberville stopped and looked over his shoulder. He spoke briefly to the small priest and walked back. Ignoring the rest of the settlers, he looked Thomas directly in the eye. "Are you the boy who saved the Mi'kmaw girl from drowning?"

Thomas's heart pounded so loudly in his ears he could barely hear. "Yes, sir," he answered.

"And your papa is not well, so you are working at Fort Royal to help your family?"

Thomas looked down at the rocks. "Yes, sir," he replied meekly.

D'Iberville turned toward his men on the beach. "This boy is an example to us all," he said loudly. "He put his own life at risk to save another. He works each day at Fort Royal to help his mama and papa. I've never heard of such bravery in one so young."

Madeleine gasped and D'Iberville looked at her and smiled. Thomas was not sure he had heard correctly. D'Iberville praising him, calling him brave?

The great soldier dug into the pocket of his long blue coat and pulled out a fat leather pouch. "This is my gift to you," he said, "to help your family. There's also plenty here for lessons with the Recollet Fathers." He placed the heavy pouch in Thomas's hands.

"Thank you, sir," said Thomas, his voice choked with emo-

tion. Lessons with the Recollet Fathers! Never had he dared dream of such a thing.

"Thomas!" exclaimed Nicolas, energetically thumping his friend on the back.

Thomas grinned at Madeleine, her eyes brimming with tears, and then at his father whose face glowed with pride. At least Madeleine and Mama would no longer need to scrub the uniforms of soldiers. Life would be easier now.

Meanwhile, D'Iberville and his party had packed into the boat and pushed away from shore. The legendary leader looked back at Thomas and smiled, raising his hand in a final salute. Thomas smiled and waved too. Then he stood on the beach with his family and friends, watching as Pierre Le Moyne Sieur D'Iberville disappeared into the morning mist.

Author's Note

Pierre Le Moyne D'Iberville returned to Plaisance (Placentia) in mid-April, 1697, and his ships from France finally arrived May 18. Onboard was a surprise for D'Iberville; he had new orders sending him back to Hudson Bay. D'Iberville left Plaisance on July 8, without ever reaching Bonavista or capturing Carbonear Island.

D'Iberville, Governor De Brouillan, Father Baudoin and William Drew were real people, and the events described about them are true. It is because of a diary kept by Father Baudoin that we know so much about D'Iberville's winter campaign.

The other people in this book are fictional, although descriptions about their lives are factual, and based on how people—including the Mi'kmaq—lived in and around Plaisance during this time. (*Mi'kmaq* refers to the plural; *Mi'kmaw* to the singular.)

In 1713, a peace agreement called the Treaty of Utrecht was signed between France and Great Britain. In it, the two countries agreed that Newfoundland belonged to Great Britain. The French retained fishing rights to part of Newfoundland's coastline, which became known as the French Shore.

Following the Treaty of Utrecht, most of the French left Placentia and moved to present-day Cape Breton, where they built the Fortress of Louisbourg.

Pierre Le Moyne D'Iberville continued his battles with the English, eventually claiming lands for France near present-day New Orleans. In July 1706, he died of yellow fever onboard his ship, while docked in Havana, Cuba. He was one week short of his 45th birthday.

During his time in Newfoundland, D'Iberville destroyed 36 settlements, captured 500 fishing boats, and 700 prisoners. Three hundred years after his death, his famous winter campaign continues to spark debate.

Bibliography

Against the Odds – A History of the Francophones of Newfoundland and Labrador, by Paul M. Charbonneau, with Louise Barrette, translation by Mike Luke, Harry Cuff Publications, St. John's, 1994.

Father Baudoin's War – D'Iberville's Campaigns in Acadia and Newfoundland 1696, 1697, by Alan F. Williams, edited by Alan G. Macpherson, Department of Geography, Memorial University of Newfoundland, St. John's, 1987.

For Maids Who Brew and Bake – Rare and Excellent Recipes from 17th Century Newfoundland, by Sheilah Roberts, Flanker Press, St. John's, 2003.

Full Circle, First Contact – Vikings and Skraelings in Newfoundland and Labrador, edited by Kevin E. McAleese, Government of Newfoundland and Labrador, St. John's, 2000.

Hopedale – Three Ages of a Community in Northern Labrador, by Carol Brice-Bennett, Historic Sites Association of Newfoundland and Labrador, St. John's, 2003.

The Military History of Placentia: A Study of the French Fortifications, by Jean-Pierre Proulx, Parks Canada, Ottawa, 1979.

Shanawdithit's People – The Archaeology of the Beothuks, by Ralph T. Pastore, Breakwater Books, St. John's, 1992.

www.currencymuseum.ca
www.collections.ic.gc.ca/placentia
www.heritage.nf.ca
www.placentia.20m.com

Many thanks to Don Short, Catherine Dempsey, Paul O'Neill, Ed Kavanagh, Jim Candow, Rob Ferguson, Don Burrage, Francois Enguehard, Eric Knight, Paul Hickey, Dwayne LaFitte, Donna Francis, Angela Pitcher, Gail Hearn, Todd Manning, Gerry Penney, Charles Martijn, Phil Jeddore, Paul Rowe, Sandy Balcom, Elizabeth Tait, Cyril Bambrick and Pat Hayward. Special thanks to our families for their continuing support.

Susan Chalker Browne
Heather Maloney